Painted Poetry

ROD MARTIN

ISBN:

(Paperback) 978-1-963565-41-6

(E-Book) 978-1-963565-42-3

Library of Congress Control Number: 2024923721

Printed in the United States of America

Published by

info@thequippyquill.com

(302) 295-2278

Dedication

This collection called "Painted Poetry" is to honor my two grand-daughters, Emily and Julia Preis. They inspire me to keep on writing poems which began over fifty years ago.

I would also like to thank the artist Vivienne Shen for coming up with the idea of putting the poems on top of paintings inspired by those poems. She provided many of the paintings for Painted Poetry with the remainder of the artwork created by the talented effort of The Quippy Quill's Production team. Thanks to Robert Williams of the production department for keeping the ball rolling on this project.

I'd like to thank all the writers out there who continue to come up with new ideas that make us think, make us laugh and make us want to join in with ideas of our own. I hope you enjoy the paintings and poetry as much as I enjoyed making this book for you.

With much Aloha,

Rod Martin

A poem for Julia:

So, I'm talking with

my grand-daughter

Two-and-a-half years old

And I say,

"How come your daddy says, Sometimes at your home

You just cry and cry and cry

But you don't cry here?"

And she says,

"That's because you're special."

And for a moment,

I was.

A poem for Emily:

If ever you feel discouraged

Or find yourself the least bit forlorn

Remember that I have loved you

Even before you were born

And I will always love you

Even when we're apart

I'll carry you with me always

Safe, right here in my heart.

One of the first poems I ever wrote:

I'm a hopeless teenager,

But I'll make it somehow.

Life is for living

and I'm gonna live mine now.

CONTENTS

For the Sake of Sound

Oh, you know…
It may seem strange
The way I can rearrange words
To say something
Or nothing at all
Like scrawl on the wall if you will, and still,
The poet is free
No, I will not be confined by my commentary
Not the least bit bound
I speak for the sake of sound
Bursting around your ear-bones
Like headphones filled with rock and roll
An imaginary stroll on a tightrope of time
and nonsense and rhyme
Just for you,

Because that's what poets do

Flutter-By

I wish I was a butterfly

And if you ever ask me "Why?"

I'd say, "I want to flutter by,

To fly on loving wings."

Yes, a Flutter-by in frolic flight
If wish you may,
Then wish you might
Wish for peace on earth
A peace so dear
Now look around.

It's here.

It's here.

A Contest With Time

Seconds race by
  Human race by the time our day is done
        we fall at the feet of forever
          begging for but a few moments more
'til…
          BANG goes the gun
              Off at a run
Chasing each moment by racing each moment
                            and it's gone

No time to mourn it
    From the day you're born it's a contest with time
      Find the reason, the rhyme
        Though you run 'til you ache with each step you take
            Desiring it
            Expiring it
Each second you take up
    Can never be made up
        So, cherish your space in the race

7

Strawflower Expectations

Crushed
    like a flower
Pressed
    between the pages of my own aching
Shattered
    by the breaking of my hope

Strawflower expectations
      having lost their living luster

Dried up
    Finding no comfort from rain-like tears
      which don't
      which I won't let flow

First flower of loving
      Plucked
        Pressed
          Unable to grow

All I Have

Love is all I have to give you

Love is all I have to give

Love is all I have

Love is all

Love is

You

Speak My Name

Where there's hope
There's fire
Here's my love
Fan the desire of my heart into flame
Speak my name
Know me completely
Memorize my touch
And never forget how much I yearn
How much I burn
To be your heart's desire
Kiss me
And learn the taste of fire

My Marvelous Mom

Great and glorious
Obviously excellent
Tremendously terrific and tender
Fabulous and fun
Amazingly awesome
Sensational and inspirational
You're a hard working woman
Witty, warm and wise
Neighborly and nice
Comforting, caring, kind
Thoughtful and thorough
Lovely and loving
Gentle, generous and genuine
Reliable and righteous
Humorous and humble
Considerate and compassionate
Fondly affectionate
Understanding, upstanding and outstanding
My marvelous Mother Dear

For Juju

So, I'm talking with my Grand-daughter

Two-and-a-half years old

And I say,

"How come your daddy says,

Sometimes, at your home you just cry and cry

But you don't cry here at our house?"

And she says,

"That's because you're special."

And for a moment,

I was.

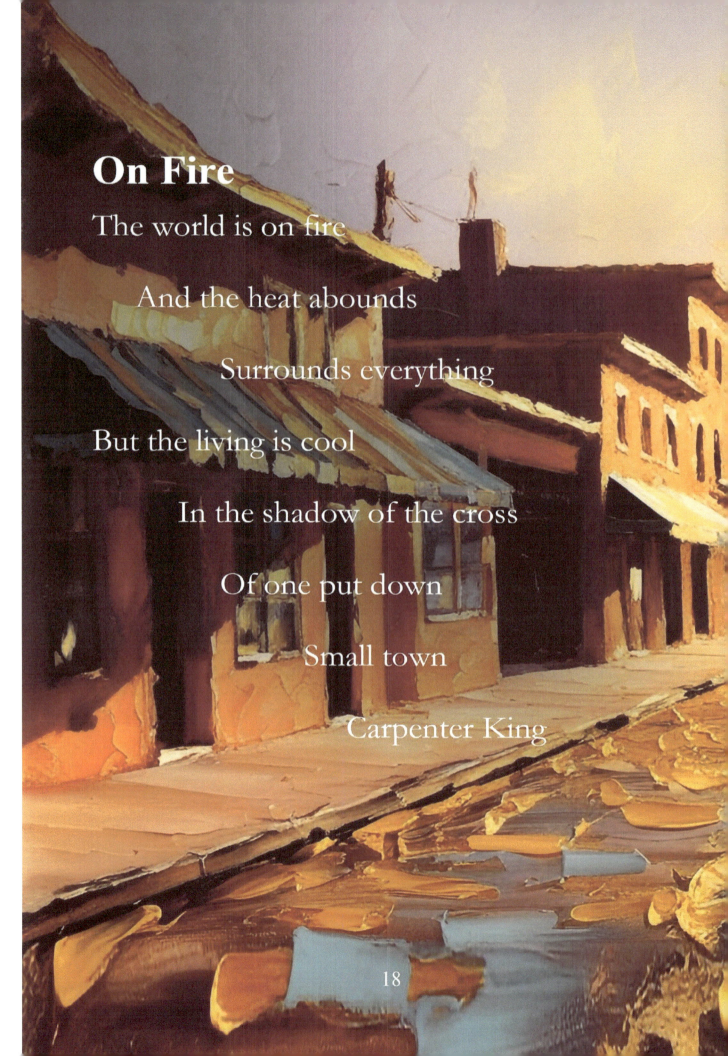

On Fire

The world is on fire

And the heat abounds

Surrounds everything

But the living is cool

In the shadow of the cross

Of one put down

Small town

Carpenter King

Straight to Jesus

Imagine me dead and by some stroke of luck
I find myself in heaven!

Not wanting to waste any time, I go straight to Jesus:

I've got a few things I've been waiting to ask you,
like, did you have to die like that?
"I didn't want to"

What about the virgin birth thing?
"They stretched things a bit when they wrote the book."

The resurrection?
"Does it really matter?"

But, the miracles?
"Exaggerations."

No walking on water, feeding the thousands, raising the dead?
"Sorry. Oh, but there is one thing that went well:

I told people to love one another…
and when they do that miracles happen."

Don't Forget Love

You can pray and preach, bow and chant
           Meditate and contemplate
You can climb mountains
      And sit surrounded by bird song breezes
         But please, don't walk away from love.
You can talk to your friends
      e-mail everyone you know
            bounce your ideas off satellites in space
               but don't forget to mention love wins.

You can be rich and famous
      Envied and pampered
         Able to buy a slice of paradise
            But my advice is to spend some time
               Looking for the loving thing.
                  Then sing, dance, sculpt, write
               and try to create more love
            wherever you go
         however much you can
      no matter what you do
don't forget to love.

Inhale

Every breath

Every conscious breath

Can be a meditation, of sorts

Sniffs and snorts of mother air

Which we hardly appreciate

Until it's not there

for a minute or two

If only our love for God and each other

Could become as indispensable

As air.

Rhyme Time

Poetry
Can really be
Done so easily

You can rhyme here or you can rhyme there
You can rhyme most anywhere

You can rhyme just for fun or for something to say
Some people rhyme most every which way

You can rhyme high or you can rhyme low
You can take a rhyme with you wherever you go

You can rhyme for the challenge or to pass the time
It can be silly or sassy, as long as it rhymes

You can rhyme pickles with tickles
Eat steaks with snakes
Try oodles of noodles or fresh frosted flakes

Make a wish with a fish. Chase a fly in the sky
Share hot dogs with bull frogs or eat hot apple pie

You can rhyme first thing in the morning
Or on a lazy afternoon

You can turn a rhyme into a song if you can find a tune
Sing it! Shout it! Tell everyone about it.

Can a drizzle fizzle? Does a stream dream?
You could me a poet and not even know it
Know what I mean?

Rhyming sturgeon with surgeon without any urgin'

Try nice dreams and moonlight
Ice cream and frostbite
There's nothing to it
I know you can do it

You can rhyme at a party or rhyme when you're home
just keep on rhyming and you'll end up with a poem

Poem as Prayer, Not Out There

Lord, the more I look

The more I find

Awaken my heart

Soothe my mind

Heighten my joy

Lower my pride

Be not, out there

Be here, inside.

Nursery Crimes

Twinkle Twinkle little sun

Will you cook us, everyone?

Up above the world so high

Sunscreen Daydream, we still fry

Crispy, Crusty, Skin and Bone

Holy Moly old Ozone

Twinkle Crinkle little sun

Roasty Toasty 'til we're done

A Bad Poem?

This is a bad poem
    the love in it is dried up
        the metaphor, ridiculous

    the similes are
        bent
        and broken

    the rhyme, non-existent

its helter skelter rhythm
    plays like burnt bongos

    the stanzas are
      slanted and silly

        and the whole kit and caboodle

            ends abruptly

Thesaurus Poem
By Patience Kanda (13) and Mr. M (48)

I would be happy…no

Cheerful…no

Delighted to have you by my side

But you're not here

You're absent

You're missing

I eagerly await your arrival

Your entrance

Your appearance

But I'm fearfully afraid that you may not show at all

And then you'll never see my loving loyalty

And dedicated devotion

And I would be hurt…

No, wounded

No, broken hearted.

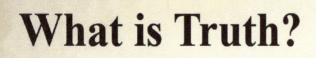

What is Truth?

What is truth?

    Who's to say?

Can truth, like man, pass away?

    If the word were carved in stone

        Mountain Big and in a line

Doesn't stone wear to dust

    amidst the test of time?

Wishes

Don't wish upon a falling star
       Or set your hopes on a heaven far
When love's the key to paradise
       And peace on earth
           Let love suffice.

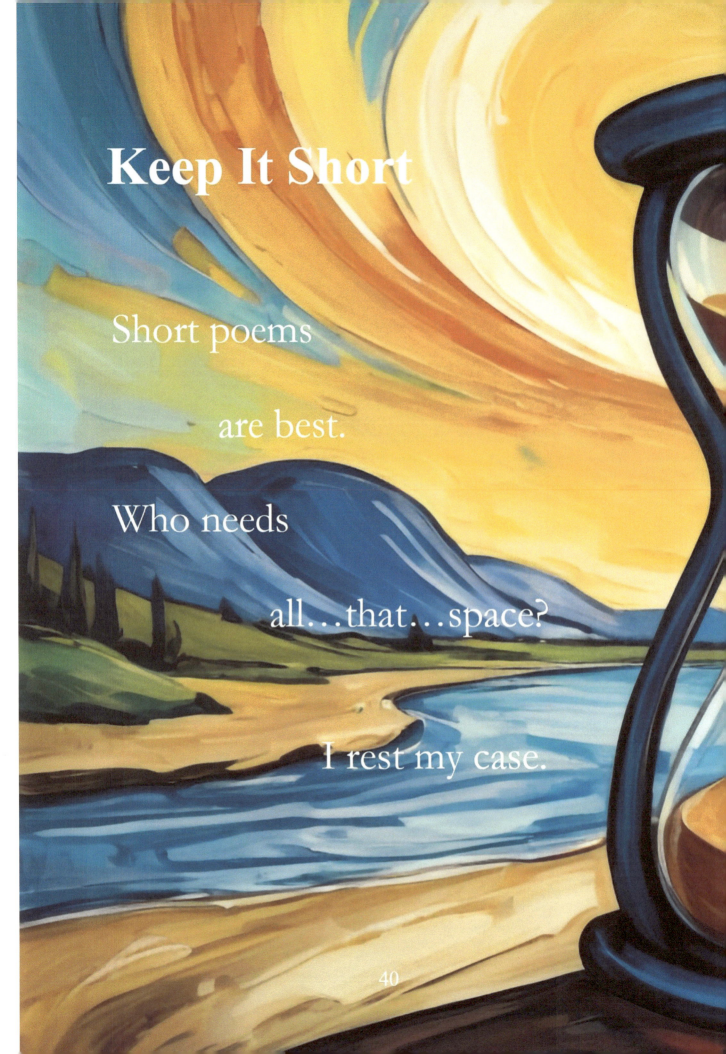

Keep It Short

Short poems

are best.

Who needs

all…that…space?

I rest my case.

41

Someday (There Will Be Love)

We're going to put away the weapons with thanks to the TV
Communication can cause changes Light illuminates, you see

And everybody's learning we get brighter all the time
And there will be a better day when we all start to shine
And the Light is Love

The world is more than nations even nature's got a song
And we could find a harmony when we learn to get along

Yes, I've seen it on my TV from a camera on the moon

A brighter day, earth rising and it's coming just as soon
Just as soon as we Love.

So you keep on hoping for a brighter day
and spread the news around
We're going to build a better world
We're not going to tear it down

We're going to be the kind of people to put an end to war

and start to live our lives in Love like we've never Loved before

Let there be Love.

Yes, Love.

Listen Carefully

It's 5:30 am

And if you listen carefully
That's when all the birds start to sing

To celebrate the coming dawn

A new day with all the possibilities you can imagine

A joyous time for reflection and peace
Surrounded by bird songs

Well worth waking up to hear
To be there

To be aware as they sing

What wonderful things this new day might bring

Braggin'

I'm a good poet. Well, not just good…
          and 'great' doesn't quite cover it.

'Outstanding' comes close,
          as does marvelous, magnificent, exquisite and amazing!

Though I prefer 'unparalleled.'

Most any superlative is always appreciated
but I don't need people singing my poetic praises
          to maintain my sense of competent accomplishment.

Frankly, words themselves fail to adequately describe
  the poetic pinnacles of satiric success I have achieved,
                                        or so I believe.

Which is in itself an ironic paradox
          since words themselves are the very tools I employ
to express my thoughts, my emotions and memories,

to describe life's mysteries,
                    to analyze, and categorize, and dramatize
each occurrence and endeavor that catches my fancy.

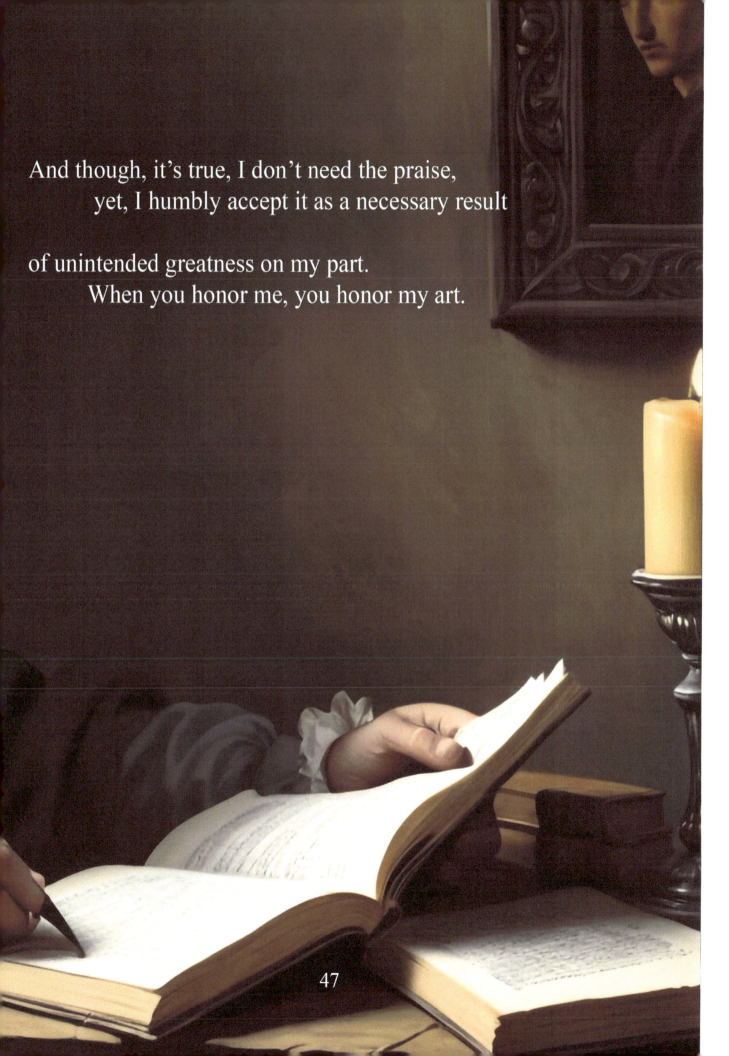

And though, it's true, I don't need the praise,
  yet, I humbly accept it as a necessary result

of unintended greatness on my part.
  When you honor me, you honor my art.

Nicknames

My first grand-daughter is just a few months old
yet in this brief span of time on earth
has acquired quite a few nicknames:

There's Sugar Plum and Baby Boo; we are so in love with you.
Lover Bug and Smiley Face: how you brighten up the place.
Big Eyes or Bright Eyes; where'd you get those Thunder Thighs?

Sleepy Peep and Fuss Button; you're so cute just doing nothin'.
Little Lizard, Snuggle Love; darling Angel from above.
Miss Bubbles, Snub Bub, Baby loves a tummy rub.

Call her all you like but she won't come
She'd rather rest and suck her thumb
Besides, she's too young to walk or run, that's all
Can't even crawl, but isn't she a Baby-doll?

Texter's Lament

Now I lay me down to text.

I have no idea what happens next.

My thumbs keep tapping, without rest,

My phone, the portal to this digital quest.

Who to message? What to say? I find my mind in disarray.

I scroll and scroll 'til my thumbs ache,

but still, I can't seem to take a break.

Connecting is key, but so is rest,

and I can't let this habit control my best.

If I wake to see the light,

I'll know I made it through the night.

but if I should die before it's sent,

I hope someone wonders where I went.

Connecticut

About the Author

Explore the literary world of Rod Martin, a multi-talented author, poet, songwriter, and playwright who lives in the lush rainforest of Kahalu'u on the Windward Side of the Island of Oahu in Hawaii. With a rich background of thirty years as an educator in Hawaii Public Schools, when Rod retired from teaching English, he dedicated his efforts to creating a diverse collection of books aimed at inspiring teachers and captivating readers.

His latest book, Painted Poetry is all about combining the words of a poem with an Artwork that it inspired. For educators seeking to infuse creativity into their classrooms, "Drama Games and Acting Exercises" is a comprehensive guide on seamlessly integrating improvisational theatre into a Language Arts curriculum. "Future Poets" opens up new horizons in the world of poetry, offering a guide for writing innovative styles.

Rod's literary repertoire extends beyond educational resources. "Jesse, Son of God" is a riveting novel, drawn from autobiographical experiences and framed as a wager between God and the Devil. His favorite novel, "Huckleberry Dick," is an enthralling love story detective mystery, featuring Joe Freedom, a private investigator, and Vana Fox, his voluptuous therapist.

Rod's first collection of poetry, "Faith, Love and Hope", recently launched on Amazon and Barnes and Noble and is followed by "Rod Martin's Poetic Madness" and "Poetic Reflections."

Not forgetting the younger audience, Rod Martin has also crafted a charming collection of children's books which include "The Tale of Natalie Nightingale," "Baby's Day," "Check This Out," "Excuses, Excuses," "The Tale of the Vorpul Snit," and "Things I Don't Know About Animals." Embark on a literary journey with Rod Martin's diverse and captivating works that span across genres, leaving a smile in the minds of readers.

Milton Keynes UK
Ingram Content Group UK Ltd.
UKHW050223021224
451695UK00002B/16